Katie Dougl

I Got Superpowers For My Birthday

Bloomsbury Methuen Drama
An imprint of Bloomsbury Publishing Plc

B L O O M S B U R Y
LONDON • OXFORD • NEW YORK • NEW DELHI • SYDNEY

Bloomsbury Methuen Drama

An imprint of Bloomsbury Publishing Plc

Imprint previously known as Methuen Drama

50 Bedford Square	1385 Broadway
London	New York
WC1B 3DP	NY 10018
UK	USA

www.bloomsbury.com

**BLOOMSBURY, METHUEN DRAMA and the Diana logo
are trademarks of Bloomsbury Publishing Plc**

First published 2016

© Katie Douglas 2016

British Library Cataloguing-in-Publication Data
A catalogue record for this book is available from the British Library.

ISBN: PB: 978-1-3500-2163-1
ePDF: 978-1-3500-2162-4
ePub: 978-1-3500-2165-5

Library of Congress Cataloging-in-Publication Data
A catalog record for this book is available from the Library of Congress

Cover design: Olivia D'Cruz
Cover image © Thread Design

Typeset by Mark Heslington Ltd, Scarborough, North Yorkshire

A Paines Plough and Half Moon production

I GOT SUPERPOWERS FOR MY BIRTHDAY

by Katie Douglas

The first performance of *I GOT SUPERPOWERS FOR MY BIRTHDAY*
took place on 5 August 2016 in Paines Plough's Roundabout
@ Summerhall, Edinburgh Festival Fringe.

Supported by
ARTS COUNCIL ENGLAND

I GOT SUPERPOWERS FOR MY BIRTHDAY

By Katie Douglas

Cast

Fiona	Remy Beasley
Ethan	Richard Corgan
William	Andy Rush
Direction	George Perrin
Lighting Design	Prema Mehta
Sound Design	Dominic Kennedy
Assistant Director	Anna Himali Howard
Dramaturgy/Creative Consultancy	Chris Elwell
Senior Producer	Hanna Streeter
Producer	Francesca Moody
Assistant Producer	Sofia Stephanou
Company Stage Manager	Caitlin O'Reilly
Technical Stage Manager	Callum Thomson
Technical Stage Manager	Hamish Ellis
Technical Director	Colin Everitt
Lighting Programmer	Peter Small
Movement Consultant	Kate Sagovsky
Costume Supervisor	Kat Smith

The play script that follows was correct at the time of going to press, but may have changed during rehearsals.

Katie Douglas (Writer)

Katie is a prize-winning scriptwriter whose work has spanned drama and comedy both here and in the States. She is a core member of the *Eastenders* writing team and previous credits include *Waterloo Road*, *Secret Diary of a Call Girl* and *Holby City*. As a playwright, she has worked with a number of theatres including Liverpool Everyman, the RSC, Paines Plough, Soho and The Royal Exchange. She was awarded the Frank Deasy Award in 2013.

Remy Beasley (Fiona)

Remy trained at Royal Welsh College of Music and Drama.

Theatre credits include: *The Insatiable, Inflatable Candylion* (National Theatre Wales), *Symphony* (nabokov/Vault Festival/Lyric Hammersmith/National Theatre Live), *Silly Kings* (National Theatre Wales), *Taming of the Shrew* (Shakespeare's Globe Theatre), *Little Dogs* (Frantic Assembly/National Theatre Wales), *nabokov Fairytales* (nabokov), *Gaslight* (Clwyd Theatr Cymru), *Love Steals Us From Loneliness* (National Theatre Wales), *It's About Time* (nabokov).

Television credits include: *Gwaith/Cartref* (Fiction Factory), *Stella* (Tidy Productions/Sky One), *Critical* (Sky One), *Perfect Summer* (BBC Wales Television).

Film credits include: *Love Is Thicker Than Water* (Mulholland Pictures + Barnsbury Pictures).

Richard Corgan (Ethan)

Richard trained at Bristol Old Vic Theatre School.

Theatre credits include: *Tom: A Story of Tom Jones –The Musical* (No.1 UK tour), *Macbeth* and *The Changeling* (Barbican Theatre, Tobacco Factory), *Press OK R&D* (Royal National Theatre), *The Merchant of Venice* (Singapore Repertory Theatre), *Gardening: For the Unfulfilled and Alienated* (Latitude Festival/Edinburgh Fringe, Fringe 1st winner), *A Provincial Life* (National Theatre Wales), *Taming of the Shrew* (Sprite Productions), *Macbeth* (Sprite Productions), *Twelfth Night* (Sprite Productions), *Taming of the Shrew* (The Globe), *Romeo & Juliet* (LCM), *Flowers From Tunisia* (Torch Theatre), *Boeing Boeing* (RCT), *Frozen, Merlin and the Cave of Dreams* (Sherman Cymru), *Othello & Cyrano De Bergerac* (Royal Opera House), *The Long, The Short and The Tall* (Pleasance, Islington), *White Devil* (Redgrave Theatre), *NSFW* (Waking Exploits).

Television credits include: *Baker Boys* (BBC Wales), series regular in *Doctors* (BBC), *Caught in the Web* (BBC), *The B-Word* (BBC Wales), *Pobol y Cwm* (S4C), *Her Majesty The Queen's 80th Birthday Party at the Palace* (BBC, live).

Film credits include: *Canaries* (Maple Dragon), *Diana* (Ecosse Films), *Magpie* (Nowhere Fast Productions).

Radio credits include: *Foursome* (BBC Radio 4), *Blue Remembered*

Hills (Christchurch Studios), *Great Ormond St Christmas Carol* (LBC).

@richardcorgan

Andy Rush (William)

Andy trained at Birmingham School of Acting.

Theatre credits include: *Tipping the Velvet* (Lyric Hammersmith), *Unidentified Item in the Bagging Area* (Pink Snail Theatre Company), *Jumpers for Goalposts* (Paines Plough), *A Midsummer Night's Dream* (The Lamb Players), *Hello/Goodbye* (Hampstead Theatre), *Love's Labour's Lost* (The Lamb Players), *The Kitchen Sink* (Bush Theatre) *Sense* (Made by Brick), *Anna Karenina* (Arcola Theatre), *Romeo & Juliet* (Cheltenham Everyman).

Television credits include: *Waterloo Road* (Headstrong Pictures), *Tommy Cooper: Not Like That, Like This* (Left Bank Pictures), *Wizards vs Aliens* (BBC), *New Tricks* (Wall to Wall).

Film credits include: *ID2: Shadwell Army* (Parrallax Pictures), *Here & Now* (Small But Tall Films Ltd).

George Perrin (Direction)

George is joint Artistic Director of Paines Plough and was formerly joint Artistic Director of nabokov. Directing credits for Paines Plough include: *Love, Lies and Taxidermy* by Alan Harris, *Growth* by Luke Norris, *I Got Superpowers For My Birthday* by Katie Douglas (Roundabout Season 2016, Edinburgh Festival Fringe and National Tour), *Every Brilliant Thing* by Duncan Macmillan with Jonny Donahoe (National and

International Tour / Barrow Street Theater, New York), *The Silver Drills* by Robin French (BBC Radio 3), *Lungs* by Duncan Macmillan, *The Human Ear* and *The Initiate* by Alexandra Wood, *Our Teacher's a Troll* by Dennis Kelly (Roundabout Season 2014/15, Edinburgh Festival Fringe and National Tour), *Not the Worst Place* by Sam Burns (Sherman Cymru / Theatr Clwyd), *Sea Wall* by Simon Stephens (Dublin Theatre Festival / National Theatre Shed), *Good with People* by David Harrower (59East59 Theatres New York / Traverse Theatre / Oran Mor), *London* by Simon Stephens (National Tour), *Sixty Five Miles* by Matt Hartley (Hull Truck), *The 8th* by Che Walker and Paul Heaton (Latitude Festival / Barbican / Manchester International Festival / National Tour), *DIG* by Katie Douglas (Oran Mor / National Tour) and *Juicy Fruits* by Leo Butler (Oran Mor / National Tour).

As Trainee Associate Director of Paines Plough, directing credits include: *House of Agnes* by Levi David Addai, *The Dirt Under the Carpet* by Rona Munro, *Crazy Love* by Che Walker, *My Little Heart Dropped in Coffee* by Duncan Macmillan and *Babies* by Katie Douglas.

Further directing credits include: *2nd May 1997* by Jack Thorne (Bush Theatre), *Terre Haute* by Edmund White (59East59 Theatres New York, West End, National Tour and Assembly Rooms, Edinburgh Festival Fringe), *Is Everyone OK?* and *Public Displays of Affection* by Joel Horwood and *Camarilla* by Van Badham (nabokov).

Prema Mehta (Lighting Design)

Prema Mehta graduated from the Guildhall School of Music and Drama.

She has designed the lighting for over 100 drama and dance productions and installations across the UK including: *Maaya* (Westminster Hall), *Bells* (Mayor of London's outdoor festival, Showtime), *Wipers* (Leicester Curve Theatre and UK tour), *Coming Up* and *Jefferson's Garden* (Watford Palace Theatre), *With a Little Bit of Luck* (Latitude Festival and UK tour), *The Dishonoured* nominated for The Offies' Best New Play (Arcola and UK tour), *The Massacre* (Theatre Royal, Bury St Edmonds), *Hercules* by New Art Club (Nottingham Playhouse and UK tour), *Red Snapper* (Belgrade Theatre, Coventry), *The Great Extension* (Theatre Royal Stratford East), *Snow Queen* (Derby Theatre), *The Electric Hills* (Liverpool Everyman), *Sufi Zen* (Royal Festival Hall) and *Dhamaka* (O2 Arena).

Prema's design work for the A-List party area at Madame Tussauds in London is open to the public throughout the year.

Current and forthcoming lighting designs include *Lady Anna: All At Sea*, directed by Colin Blumenall, and *Spring Awakening*, directed by Nikolai Foster.

Full credits and production gallery can be viewed at www.premamehta.com

Dominic Kennedy (Sound Design)

Dominic Kennedy is a sound designer and music producer for performance and live events. He has a keen interest in developing new work and implementing sound and music at an early stage in a creative process. Dominic is a graduate from Royal Central School of Speech and Drama where he developed specialist skills in collaborative and devised theatre making, music composition and installation practices. His work often fuses found sound, field recordings, music composition and synthesis. Dominic has recently designed for and collaborated with Paines Plough, Goat and Monkey, Jamie Wood, Gameshow, Manchester Royal Exchange, Engineer, Outbox, Jemima James and Mars Tarrab. Recent installation work includes interactive sound design for Gingerline (pop-up restaurant pioneers) and the launch of Terry Pratchett's *The Shepherd's Crown*.

Recent theatre credits include: *With a Little Bit of Luck* (nationwide tour), *The Human Ear* (Roundabout), *The Devil Speaks True* (The Vaults and nationwide tour), *Run* (New Diorama), *ONO* (Soho Theatre), *Our Teacher's a Troll* (Roundabout), *Crocodiles* (Manchester Royal Exchange), *Karagular* (Shoreditch Town Hall).

Anna Himali Howard (Assistant Director)

Anna is a theatremaker and director who graduated from the University of Warwick in 2015. Prior to joining

Paines Plough, Anna was a performer and deviser in Breach Theatre's *The Beanfield,* which received a Total Theatre Award at the Edinburgh Fringe in 2015 and toured nationally in 2016. She is a Creative Associate at the Gate Theatre, where she assistant directed *In the Night Time (Before the Sun Rises)* by Nina Segal, and an alumnus of the REP Foundry artist development scheme. Other credits include *Life Is No Laughing Matter* by Demi Nandhra as director (Battersea Arts Centre, Normal? Festival) and *20B* by Jane English as dramaturg (Birmingham REP, Theatre Royal Stratford East).

Chris Elwell (Dramaturg/Creative Consultant)

Chris is the Director/CEO of Half Moon Theatre, London. He is a director/writer, trainer and theatre producer specialising in professional theatre for young audiences. He has a strong track record in the development and delivery of work with a particular emphasis upon inclusion particularly in the field of cultural and disability diversity, and socio-economic disfranchisement. Chris has directed over thirty pieces of work for family, teenage and community audiences. Most recent directing credits include *Free* by David Lane, *When Spring Comes* (devised), *Moon and Genie* by Tanika Gupta, *Big Red Bath* (adapted by Chris Elwell), *Rip, Fold, Scrunch* (devised), as well as a cannon of work in English and British Sign Language which Chris wrote and directed, including: *Baa Moo Yellow Dog* (also adapted for TV in 2010), *Icicle Bicycle, Igloo Hullabaloo and My Friend Snow.* Most recently he has directed a series of spoken word theatre pieces including Big Wow Small Wonder and Fairytales Gone Bad.

Chris is the curator of Exchange for Change sector significant artform development programme that challenges perceptions of the work produced in the young people's sector. This extensive programme particularly engages artists from non-theatre backgrounds (design, digital/new media, dance, spoken word etc.), those who are under-represented in the sector and emerging young people's theatre companies. Much of this work tours nationally and internationally through Half Moon Presents, the company's producing arm.

Paines Plough

Paines Plough is the UK's national theatre of new plays. We commission and produce the best playwrights and tour their plays far and wide. Whether you're in Liverpool or Lyme Regis, Scarborough or Southampton, a Paines Plough show is coming to a theatre near you soon.

"The lifeblood of the UK's theatre ecosystem" *The Guardian*

Paines Plough was formed in 1974 over a pint of Paines bitter in the Plough pub. Since then, we've produced more than 130 new productions by world-renowned playwrights like Stephen Jeffreys, Abi Morgan, Sarah Kane, Mark Ravenhill, Dennis Kelly and Mike Bartlett. We've toured those plays to hundreds of places from Manchester to Moscow to Maidenhead.

"That noble company Paines Plough, de facto national theatre of new writing" *The Daily Telegraph*

Our Programme 2015 saw 12 productions by the nation's finest writers touring to 84 places from Cornwall to the Orkney Islands; in village halls and Off-Broadway, at music festivals and student unions, online and on radio, and in our own pop-up theatre Roundabout.

With Programme 2016, we continue to tour the length and breadth of the UK from clubs and pubs to lakeside escapes and housing estates. Roundabout hosts our most ambitious Edinburgh Festival Fringe programme ever and brings mini-festivals to each stop on its Autumn tour. We're extending our digital reach by live streaming shows and launching our free Come To Where I'm From app featuring over 100 audio plays.

"I think some theatre just saved my life" *@kate_clement on Twitter*

"A beautifully designed masterpiece in engineering... a significant breakthrough in theatre technology." The Stage

Roundabout is Paines Plough's beautiful portable in-the-round theatre. It's a completely self-contained 168-seat auditorium that flat-packs into a lorry and can pop up anywhere from theatres to school halls, sports centres, warehouses, car parks and fields.

We built Roundabout to enable us to tour to places that don't have theatres. For the next decade, Roundabout will travel the length and breadth of the UK bringing the nation's best playwrights and a thrilling theatrical experience to audiences everywhere.

In 2015 alone, Roundabout played host to 380 hours of activity, including more than 200 performances by Paines Plough. Over 25,000 people saw a show in Roundabout.

Roundabout was designed by Lucy Osborne and Emma Chapman at Studio Three Sixty in collaboration with Charcoalblue and Howard Eaton.

WINNER of Theatre Building of the Year at The Stage Awards 2014

"The @painesplough Roundabout venue wins most beautiful interior venue by far @edfringe."
@ChaoticKirsty on Twitter

"Roundabout is a beautiful, magical space. Hidden tech make it Turkish-bath-tranquil but with circus-tent-cheek. Aces."
@evenicol on Twitter

Roundabout was only made possible thanks to the belief and generous support of the following Trusts and individuals. We thank them all.

TRUSTS AND FOUNDATIONS
Andrew Lloyd Webber Foundation
Paul Hamlyn Foundation
Garfield Weston Foundation
J Paul Getty Jnr Charitable Trust
John Ellerman Foundation

CORPORATE
Universal Consolidated Group
Howard Eaton Lighting Ltd
Charcoalblue
Avolites Ltd
Factory Settings
Total Solutions

Pop your name on a seat and help us pop-up around the UK: www.
justgiving.com/fundraising/roundaboutauditorium

www.painesplough.com/roundabout

#roundaboutpp

Half Moon

Half Moon is the UK's leading small-scale young people's venue and touring company, with the local community at the heart of its ethos. Half Moon is a local organisation with a national remit, committed to supporting artists and young people at every stage of their creative development. Working from their base in East London, Half Moon specialise in new writing and artform development, acting as a gateway organisation that provides pathways for progression and experimentation. Their wide-ranging programme reaches nearly 50,000 people annually and engages those who are often excluded from arts activity. Their activity includes seasons of professional plays for young audiences, national touring productions and an extensive creative learning programme, including seven youth theatres. This is Half Moon's second co-production with Paines Plough, having preciously collaborated on *Our Teacher's A Troll* in 2014 and 2015. Half Moon is a National Portfolio Organisation of Arts Council England and receives regular funding from the London Borough of Tower Hamlets. Half Moon's digital archive is available at www.stagesofhalfmoon.org.uk.

Half Moon Young People's Theatre is a company limited by guarantee and a registered charity.

Registered Company no: 2479179
Registered Charity no: 1010192

Half Moon Theatre, 43 White Horse Road, London E1 0ND
+ 44 (0) 20 7709 8900
admin@halfmoon.org.uk
www.halfmoon.org.uk

Follow @HalfMoonTheatre on Twitter
Like Half Moon at facebook.com/HalfMoonTheatre
Donate to Half Moon at *www.halfmoon.org.uk/support-us*

Half Moon are:

Beccy Allen	Producer (Creative Learning)
Phil Clarke	Production and Technical Manager
Euan Borland	Venue and Programmes Administrator
John Bunker	Cleaner
Jackie Eley	Administrative Director
Chris Elwell	Director/CEO
Stephen Beeny	Communications Manager

Board of Directors:

Julian Sutton (Chair/Treasurer), Duncan Holden (Vice Chair), Dawn Harrison-Wallace, Sarah Haworth, Anuradha Laws, Elaine McLaughlin, Orla Sanders, Martin Welton, Julia Williams, Penny Wrout

I Got Superpowers For My Birthday

Our Heroes

Ethan
Fiona
William

All three of them are turning thirteen today.

All other parts to be played by the company.

Fiona So I wake up –

Ethan Mum brings me toast and jam as usual.

Fiona Monday. I *hate* Mondays.

William Except it's not just any Monday.

Fiona So what if it's my birthday? Not like there's anyone around to care.

William Dad's laid out my cards on the table, all ready and waiting for me.

Ethan Mum's more excited than I am as she watches me open my presents. Course I already know what she's got me. She hides stuff *really badly*.

William We both know I won't get what I really want for my birthday. But a computer game and DVDs are pretty good too. (*To his Dad.*) Thanks, Dad.

Ethan (*to his Mum*) A new pair of headphones! Awesome, Mum!

Fiona Auntie Bev shoves a digestive biscuit at me as I walk out the door. Some birthday this is turning out to be.

Ethan But *why* do I have to go to school? It's my birthday!

William Run to school. Hate being late.

Fiona Wander in – Hello, World!

William Sit at the front of the class.

Fiona No one answers. Stuff you, World.

Ethan High-fives from all the guys on my way in.

Ethan *gives all his gang high-fives.*

William 'Nerd!' shouts one of the lads from the back. I ignore it.

Ethan   'Why do you always have to be the centre of attention?' asks the teacher, Mrs Boyd. She's totally got it in for me.

Fiona   The first two rows are filled with the hair girls, as I call them. In one hand a mirror, in the other a brush. Upstairs? The lights are on but they're not that bright if you get what I'm saying.

William   'Ethan?'

Ethan   Here, Miss! 'Fiona?'

Fiona   Here, Miss! 'William?'

William   Obviously I'm here, Miss! Like I'd miss school on library day . . .

Ethan (*with pride*)   Course all anyone can talk about is the party of the century.

Fiona   What is this party everyone keeps banging on about?

Ethan   Mum sent the invites out ages ago.

William   Maybe mine got lost in the post?

Fiona   Like I'd want to go to some stupid party anyway!

William   Cos we're totally sort of mates.

Ethan   *All* my mates have been invited. Literally no one I care about has been forgotten.

William   Probably just some sort of mix-up.

Fiona   If I wanted a party I'd have my own party.

William   Dad didn't feel much like celebrating this year but it'd be nice to be around candles and cake and balloons and all that stuff. (*Beat; hopeful.*) Maybe I'll just show up?

Ethan   Strictly no gatecrashers!

William It's not like anyone would turn me away. I'm adorable. (*Beat; tinge of sadness.*) At least that's what my Mum always used to say.

Fiona We get to maths. It's finally time to unearth that digestive from my pocket and chow down.

William Favourite lesson of the day.

Ethan *Worst lesson of the day.* When's it time for music?

Fiona Lunch.

William Wonder what I'm going to wear to the party? It's gonna have to be something special.

Ethan When will I start to feel different?

William This is not just any birthday.

Fiona It's no big deal.

Ethan Mum says I'll always be her little soldier.

William Thirteen is mega.

Fiona Just another Monday.

Ethan But from now on, I'm my own man. (*Beat.*) The start of something.

William The start of something.

Fiona It could have been the start of something.

Pause.

Ethan/Fiona/William Turning thirteen is no joke.

William *runs into* **Ethan** *as he's coming the other way.* **Ethan's** *bag goes flying.*

Ethan Watch it!

William *bends down to help* **Ethan** *pick up his things.*

William So thirteen, yeah?

Ethan   What's it got to do with you?

William   It's just – y'know, everyone's talking about the party and I thought . . .

Ethan   *Nothing to do with you.*

William   It could be, though?

Ethan   Invites have gone out.

William   Always room for one more!

Ethan   Mum's only ordered a cake the exact right size, so . . .

William   Hate cake. So no problem!

Ethan   Mate . . .

William   Aha! So you admit we're mates, then?

Ethan   Mate, get the message.

Ethan *has all his stuff. He shoulders his bag.*

Ethan   We only ever got stuck hanging out together cos our Mums knew each other and now, well . . .

Ethan *doesn't need to say it. This is awkward.*

Ethan   Your Mum's not around anymore, is she?

William *is quiet for a beat.*

William   She's coming back.

Ethan *shakes his head.*

William   She is.

Ethan   Whatever . . .

William   She is!

Ethan *tuts, not believing a word of it.*

William   My Mum's coming back for me. I don't care what anyone says.

William *walks away and sits down on his own.*

Ethan (*shouting after him*)   Just stay away from me, yeah?

Fiona   Why can't you just say she's coming back?

Ethan *looks at* **Fiona** *and shakes his head.*

Ethan   Who are you anyway? I don't even know you.

Fiona   Yeah, we've only been at school together since we were five. I can see how you might have missed me.

Ethan   What are you getting on my back for?

Fiona   Just trying to have a conversation.

Ethan   I don't get you. Either of you!

Fiona *walks away and sits down on her own.*

Ethan   Weirdos.

After a beat, **Ethan** *goes and sits down on his own too.*

Fiona   Home again.

William   Dad works.

Ethan   Mum's waiting.

Fiona   Auntie Bev's . . . (*In disbelief.*) You're watching Frozen – again??!!

William   I make myself one of those microwave pizzas.

Ethan   Homework. Mum's, like, obsessed.

Fiona   Auntie Bev, you are not Elsa! You're a forty-five year old woman with a perm!

William   Ah! Too hot!

Ethan   This should be banned. Maths on my birthday?!

Fiona   Time to put the spuds on for dinner.

William   Video games for a few hours.

Ethan   Thirty minutes of guitar practice straight after.

Fiona   Radio on. Time for a break-out dance.

Fiona *does a break-out dance.*

William   Grenade attack! Duck!

William *does a forward roll and ducks behind a sofa.*

Ethan   Rocking out a new riff.

Fiona (*shouting*)   Auntie Bev! Dinner!

Ethan   Macaroni cheese. Wicked – thanks, Mum.

William   Dad's home late. Straight to bed.

Ethan   I think she's more excited about the party than I am.

William   He doesn't spend as much time out of bed as he used to.

Ethan   Go to my room –

Fiona   Winding down.

William   Chilling out.

Ethan   Dreaming that I'm in a world-conquering rock band – Hello, Wembley!

William   Wishing Mum would come home –

Fiona   Nothing – then –

Ethan, **William** *and* **Fiona** *all wake up at the same time.*

William   I hear a noise.

Ethan   What was that?

Fiona   Could be the wind.

William   Dad's in the other room. Could have been him?

Ethan   Didn't sound like a sound Mum would make.

Fiona   Auntie Bev isn't subtle. She makes noise, you know she's making it.

William   Pretty sure he's asleep, though . . .

Ethan   Could be . . . a cat?

William   When I was little I used to be afraid of monsters. I'd make Mum check in every wardrobe in the house before I'd go to sleep.

Fiona   There it is again! Louder, this time.

William   We'd go round every room, look in every door. Last thing – under the bed.

Fiona   Definitely something there.

Ethan   Please be a cat, please be a cat, please be a cat.

William   Lucky I don't believe in monsters anymore.

Ethan   Smash! There it is.

Fiona   See it out the corner of my eye. Filthy –

William   Gross. Covered in slime.

Fiona   One eye all like . . .

Fiona *does an impression of a really gross-looking eyeball hanging out of its socket.*

Ethan   So I shout for Mum –

Fiona   Go at it with a spanner –

William   Hide. Under the covers. Right up to the neck so I'm safe. Cos that's the rule, right? (*Beat; worried.*) It is the rule, yeah?

Fiona   Smack it and it goes flying. Boing! Right across the room.

Ethan   Mum comes running. She's always listening out for me in case I need something. Usually it's juice or something not, y'know – back-up.

William   Dad's down the hall.

Fiona   Back-up, smack-up! Look at that thing run!

William   I want him to come and get me. *(Shouting.)* Dad!

Fiona   I do a victory dance.

Fiona does a victory dance.

William *(shouting even louder)*   Dad!

Ethan   Grab a softball bat from in the cupboard!

William *(with growing fear)*   Dad! Dad!

Fiona   It comes back at me. Woosh! I duck out the way just in time. I reach for the spanner again but instead – fire from my fingertips! What?! The flame shoots right at the gargoyle and fries him into a crispy critter right in front of my eyes. He tries to run but his legs are charcoal. They crumble into bits as he dashes for the door and I've got to finish him off, haven't I, so I point my fingers in his direction again, more fire shoots out, and the gargoyle falls onto the carpet looking like a bit of crispy bacon. Course Auntie Bev's new throw pillow gets caught in the cross-fire. I'll have to explain that one later . . .

Ethan *starts beating the gargoyle with his bat.*

Ethan *(in time with the blows)*   Stay. Down. Creepy. Gargoyle. Thing. Why. Won't. You. Die?! *(Beat.)* I chuck the bat to one side – clearly not working – and the ground shifts beneath my feet. I put my hand to the carpet and the earth beneath rumbles. More and more as I focus on what I have to do. It's working! The gargoyle can't stay stood up – the whole room is shaking! A trophy from the shelf is going wibble wobble back and forth and back and forth until – flop! It dives off the shelf and smacks the gargoyle right on the head, killing him dead. Victory!

Fiona   What sort of strange, pointy-headed, green-around-the-gills creature was that? And since when can I shoot fire from my fingertips?! Is that going to happen every time I reach for something? That doesn't sound practical. I'll, like, always have burned toast!

Ethan   I shake the ground just in case there's any more nasties about to come and attack. 'What was that?' says Mum. 'Just a couple of big farts!' I shout back. 'Sorry, Mum, couldn't hold them in!'

Pause.

William   He's not coming. Can't he hear me?

Fiona   This is weird.

Ethan   *So* weird.

William   I get out of bed. Walk down the hall.

Fiona   Why are evil gargoyles after me? And as for the fire thing . . .

Ethan   How did I do that?!

William   Dad! (*Beat.*) Nothing. Something's wrong. The whole house is . . . dark. Creepy. *Dank.* His room's straight ahead now. Lights off. A lump in bed like always. I feel better but – why isn't he moving? He should be able to *see* me by now. Dad? (*Beat.*) The gargoyle must have taken him by surprise cos he looks peaceful lying there. Dad turned to face the picture of the three of us on his bedside table. Me, Mum and Dad before it all went wrong and she had to go. (*Beat.*) You'd never know he was dead if it wasn't for his eyes. A gargoyle comes dashing out from under the bed. I kick it into the air, I stare at it and suddenly it's frozen solid! The gargoyle falls to the ground and smashes into a thousand pieces. Kill my Dad, will you?! Then – Dad leaps up, all like 'Ah!' and I'm like 'Ah!' and he goes 'AH!' and I . . . You get the picture. Dad, I thought you were – you *looked* –

William *can't bring himself to complete the sentence.*

William   Dad looks at me and he says – 'I saw something. A strange little creature with spikey things on his head and loads of extra skin. It hit me in the face with a wet flannel! Must have picked it up from the bathroom . . . What do you reckon that could have been then?' I think about it for a second, figuring out what to say. I can't tell him the truth so I go, 'Bad dream?' What is happening to me? Why can I make things turn to ice with just a look?

Fiona   I'm awake half the night worrying about what just happened but eventually I fall asleep.

Ethan   Part of me thinks it was just a strange dream but a bigger part knows it was real.

Fiona   The alarm clock goes off. School time.

Ethan   Same again.

William   Except different. Everything's different now.

Fiona   I walk to school, on the look-out for any weird creatures that might attack from nowhere.

Ethan   Bit on edge, if I'm honest.

William   Last night was . . . strange. To say the least.

Fiona   The fire from the fingertips is new.

Ethan   Pretty chuffed at how I made the ground rumble with just a touch.

William   Freezing things with just a look? Awesome.

Ethan   The world is full of possibilities.

Fiona   *Fun* possibilities.

Ethan   I can do anything!

Fiona   Well, one thing mainly.

Ethan   Anything to do with the earth anyway.

William   Water.

Fiona   Fire.

Ethan   Don't know why. Or how long it'll last.

William   Lunchtime.

Fiona   They're all in the dining hall. The other kids. *Popular* kids.

William   Playing football.

Fiona   Pizza day so the queues are, like, insane.

Ethan   Every Tuesday lunchtime it's extra maths practice.

William   No one ever picks me for their team.

Ethan   I hate maths and I'm no good at it, but no way would Mum let me quit.

William   Even though I love football. Even though I'm probably better than any of them.

Fiona   Girls all chatting. Boys all shouting.

William (*to the lads*)   Can I play?

Ethan   So sick of equations.

William   They say yes! But then – hang on a minute . . .

Ethan   Who needs to know how to do fractions anyway?

William   In goal?! No one wants to be in goal!

Ethan   Rather be strumming a guitar.

William   The one position I can't play. I take up my stance and things get started.

Ethan   Still, nothing worse than being asked a question and not knowing the answer. No one wants *that*.

William   One of them kicks, another one dribbles. Someone looks like they're about to score.

Fiona   The noise levels in there are getting mad. And they all only want one thing. The magic cheese and tomato. The mighty pizza!

William   He's running down the wing – legging it like lightning –

Fiona (*chanting*)   Pizza, pizza, pizza.

The rest of the kids join in.

Everyone   Pizza, pizza, pizza.

Fiona   A bunch of the hair girls get to the front. They're practically drooling. They can *see* it – *taste* it –

William   There's only one way I'm stopping him from getting a goal.

Fiona   I bide my time . . .

William   I crouch for extra balance . . .

Ethan   I am *rubbish* at this stuff.

Fiona   Wait until she reaches out for the yummy doughy crust –

William   I'm barely breathing as he swings his leg back –

Fiona   Her hand's inches away –

Ethan   The teacher asks another question. Everyone else has answered one except for me.

William   He's just about to kick it when – I fix my eyes on the ground and turn the whole pitch to a sheet of ice! Everyone's scrambling around, slippy sliding . . . In all the chaos I grab the ball – what a save!

Fiona   Sorry, ladies, your pizza is burned to a cinder . . .

Ethan   Earthquake! Everyone falls to the ground which gives me just enough time to dash over to Miss Potts' desk and check the answer. By the time they've recovered my hand's in the air. 'I've got the answer for you, Miss!'

Fiona   Brush your hair for twenty hours a day and ignore everyone else, will you? No pizza today!

Ethan/Fiona/William   Having superpowers is amazing!!

Fiona   Until Mrs Katz says, 'We don't know how you did it, Fiona, but you gave yourself away by laughing at the incident in the cafeteria. The dinner ladies think maybe you tampered with the oven.'

Ethan   'I know you cheated in maths practice,' Miss Potts says.

William   'How did you do it?' asks the PE teacher, Mr Willis. 'Pour water onto the pitch, did you? It's pretty cold out there – someone could have broken a leg on all that ice.' If only he knew how I'd really done it . . .

Fiona   'Detention!'

Ethan   'Detention!'

William   'Detention!'

Fiona   So come half three that's where I head. Detention. It's always held in the gym hall, which is so big and freezing that it's the stuff of nightmares. They put a few desks in there after school for all the detention crew – uncomfy chairs where kids can sit and write lines or do homework or whatever they've been assigned to do to fill the forty-five minutes they're allowed to keep us for.

Ethan   Hate detention.

William   Mr Collins the Chemistry teacher is supposed to be looking after us but he keeps nipping back to his office every two minutes to get more marking.

Fiona   Have a sneaky cigarette, more like . . .

Ethan   'Don't move a muscle!' Mr Collins says. 'I've got eyes in the back of my head!'

Fiona   It'll be hard for those eyes to see through the cloud of stinky smoke you're about to start creating . . . Off he goes, closing the door behind him.

William   Which means I'm stuck looking at *them*.

Ethan   Bit awkward after what I said about his Mum.

Fiona   For the first time ever, being in detention doesn't seem so bad.

William   At least it gives me time to think.

Ethan   Loads on my mind. Like, y'know, where did these superpowers come from?

Fiona   Why now?

William   Why me?

Fiona   I've always felt different, so this is nothing new. Auntie Bev's always saying to me – 'Fiona, you've been paddling your own canoe from the day you were born. Why not let the world take over a bit?' but that's not in my nature, I say to her. I'm a lone wolf, a pioneer, a fly by the seat of her pants type that goes boldly where no one's bothered to go before and that's just the way I like it. (*Beat.*) Except . . . The truth is, it'd be nice not to be on my own so much. To feel part of something for a change. It'd be good if when people saw me they were like 'Oh that's Fiona. You know her, she's on the netball team' or 'Fiona. You know the one! She's got loads of brothers and sisters, I don't know how she copes.' They don't say any of that, though, because I'm not. I'm just me. Having superpowers is only going to make me seem more unusual. 'Shall we make friends with Fiona? She lives with her Auntie who's a dinner lady and, oh yeah, she can shoot fire from her fingers and make flames dance at her command.' Doesn't sound likely, does it?

Ethan   Maybe these powers are like a tummy virus. In a few days they'll just go away on their own?

William   Can't *believe* I'm stuck in a room with these two.

Fiona   Best just keep my head down, copy out these lines like I'm supposed to and –

Ethan   What was that?

Fiona   We all spin round to look at the same bit of the room, so you know we all must have heard the same thing.

William   Noise. Sounded like a crash.

Fiona   There it goes again! The same sound. Getting a bit scary now.

Ethan   Not another gargoyle thing . . .

William *and* **Fiona** *look at* **Ethan** *sharply.*

Fiona   *What* did you just say?

Ethan (*innocent*)   Nothing.

William   'Not another gargoyle thing.'

Fiona   *Another* gargoyle.

William   Which means you've seen a gargoyle before.

Ethan   It's nothing.

Fiona   He's lying.

Ethan   I'm not! There wasn't anything! Not a thing! I absolutely definitely did not see a –

Fiona   Ah!

William   There it is again!

Fiona   A thump and crash and something scuttles out from one of the other desks.

Ethan   GARGOYLE!

Fiona   You saw a gargoyle?!

Ethan (*playing it cool*)   Pfft. No. What makes you say that?

William   Did it look like this?

William *does an impression of a really ugly-looking gargoyle.*

Fiona   Don't forget the . . .

Fiona *does an impression of a gross-looking eye hanging out of its socket.*

William   Wait a minute . . .

William/Fiona   *You saw one too?!*

Ethan   Well I don't know what you two saw but I didn't see a thing.

Fiona   You can drop the act now – we clearly all saw one?

Ethan   One what?

William/Fiona   A gargoyle!

Ethan   'I'm not a gargoyle.'

William/Fiona   Ahhh!

Ethan   'I'm a goblin,' goes the creature. 'There are several key differences between your gargoyles and your goblins. Number one – we smell of fresh fruits while those horrible gargoyles stink of feet. And not just any old feet. Wet feet. Wet old man feet . . .'

William (*scared*)   Great time to be in your office, Mr Collins . . .

Ethan   'Number two – gargoyles have a terrible diet and will eat any old thing,' the critter goes on. 'Cats, rubber rings, bits of old cassette tapes – you name it. We goblins on the other hand are very discerning creatures.'

Fiona   So what do you lot eat then?

A beat.

Ethan   He opens his mouth wide, saliva dripping from his lips like rain and says – '*Children.*'

William/Fiona   Ahhh!

Fiona   I think fast. How did I get rid of that gargoyle again?

William   Turning a football pitch to ice is one thing, but fighting a goblin? I'm not ready for that!

Ethan   But what choice is there? I have to try.

Fiona   Fire from the fingertips! Worked on gargoyle guy, should work on goblin man.

William   I focus on the goblin. Stare him down. I think freeze freeze freeze!

Ethan   Yowp!

William   Oops, Ethan got in the way. Sorry!

Ethan   Why is my bum freezing cold?!

William   I *knew* I wasn't ready . . .

Ethan   I want to try and make the ground so wibbly wobbly the goblin can't stay standing but I can't get my hand to the ground anywhere near him. He keeps moving!

Fiona   I point my finger at the goblin. Think hot thoughts and . . . It's working! Flames shoot from the ends of my nails and in two seconds flat the goblin's feet are hotter than a beach in summer. He leaps from foot to foot!

Ethan   'Oww, eee, ooh!' cries the goblin as he falls to the floor in agony.

Fiona   William and Ethan might have fumbled the ball but I am getting this thing done!

Ethan   'Stop!' the goblin wails. 'How are you doing this? You're just kids!'

William   Lucky Fiona was here, really . . .

Fiona   We gather round, look down at him and say, 'We're not kids, goblin man. We're thirteen.'

William   Now GO!

Ethan   The goblin's on his feet in two seconds flat. 'Look out,' he says, 'Goblins are nothing compared to what's coming for you next. This isn't over!' And with that he scuttles off out the gym hall.

William   And all we can do is stand there.

Fiona   Looking at each other.

Ethan   The three of us. (*Beat.*) So you can . . .

Fiona   As of yesterday, yeah. And you can . . .

Ethan   Looks that way, doesn't it? And you . . .

William   Happened the same way. Woke up.

Ethan/Fiona/William   On my birthday.

Ethan   And suddenly –

Ethan/Fiona/William   Superpowers.

Fiona   As if from –

Ethan/Fiona/William   Nowhere.

William   Only they can't have come from nowhere, can they? They have to have come from somewhere. And if there's three of us then . . .

Fiona   Our powers must have come from the same place.

They take a long minute to get their heads around that.

Ethan   I, like, barely even know these people.

Fiona   Seen them around school.

William   His Mum was mates with my Mum.

Fiona   Only said hello a few times.

Ethan   No clue who *she* is.

William   We can't be *linked* –

Fiona   Got to be some sort of mix-up . . .

Ethan   Coincidence, maybe?

Fiona   A mistake. Like when Auntie Bev got on a bus that time thinking she was going to London and ended up in Stockton-on-Tees. (*Beat.*) Superpowers don't just come on for no reason.

William   Like the mumps.

Ethan   There's *always* –

Fiona   Some kind of creepy, weird, unbelievable –

William   Reason for stuff like this happening.

Ethan   We can't handle this.

Fiona   We're *kids* –

William   Only one thing to do.

Ethan   Ignore it.

Fiona   Heads down.

William   Focus on homework and video games. Normal stuff.

Ethan   Not superhero video games, though.

William   Anything but them!

Fiona   And in the meantime –

Ethan   We stay away from each other.

William   Pretend we don't know each other.

Ethan   Should be easy.

Fiona   No problemo.

William   We say nothing, we do nothing.

Ethan   We go back to there being no such thing as monsters.

Fiona   No such thing as superpowers.

William   Boring normality, here we come!

Fiona   So I knuckle down and let the days slide past.

Ethan   Nothing much happens.

William   School, school, library, home, school . . .

Fiona   It's mainly eating digestives and watching a bit of telly, if I'm honest.

Ethan   Bit of party prep but everything's pretty much sorted.

William   I get a start on some coursework that's not due in for another six months.

Fiona   I tidy my room. Not done that in a while.

Ethan   Guitar practice.

Fiona   Auntie Bev's a bit suspicious. She reckons I've got into trouble at school or something. If only she knew . . .

Ethan   I've almost learned a whole new chord!

William   A hundred whole pages of my book read. Boom!

Fiona   I agree to watch Lion King for the millionth time just to keep her sweet.

William   Boring has never felt so good!

Fiona   Maybe this whole thing was just a blip.

Ethan   A dream.

William   After a few days I'm all like 'superpowers? What superpowers?'

Fiona   Probably just a phase.

William   And then it's the weekend . . .

Ethan   Saturday! Which means . . .

Ethan/Fiona/William   No school!

Ethan   The party of the century is about to open its doors.

William   I know I made a promise, but I can't resist going to the library to try and work out what happened to me. They've got to have a section called 'superpowers, gargoyles and other strange things that happen to thirteen year olds', right? I head to the door but Dad's blocking me. 'Hang on, young man, where d'you think you're going?' Dad's spent the last six months in bed. *Now* he decides to start asking where I'm going?! I say – 'The library, Dad. Homework. Loads and loads of really, properly hard homework.'

Fiona   I know I made a promise not to use my powers and everything but the toaster's on the blink again.

William   'It's a Saturday,' Dad says. 'You don't want to be going to the library on a Saturday.' (*Beat.*) Unbelievable!

Ethan   I've got to get this place ready for the party. (*Beat.*) Shame I can't use my superpowers to blow up 200 balloons . . .

Fiona   I've no idea how the toast got burned, Auntie Bev, it's on the same setting as usual. Have a digestive biscuit instead, go on.

William   I have to go, Dad! (*Beat.*) Grab my bag. Run for the door. He blocks me! 'I know I've been a bit . . . down since your Mum left,' he starts saying. 'But I also know that things have to change. You've been my priority ever since you came to live with us and I can't let that change now.'

William *sighs.*

William   How can I run off when he's saying all this nice stuff? 'How about we start by getting out the house?' There he goes again . . . 'Your friend Ethan's having a party later.' *Not* my friend Ethan, I want to say. 'His Mum said we should pop along. How about it?'

William *shakes his head.*

William   No way! (*Beat.*) Is what I *should* say. But I can't let Dad down when he's trying so hard, so I go: 'What time do you want to set off?'

Fiona   Saturdays in our house are awesome. Auntie Bev works at the community centre all day which means it's just me, the TV and a full packet of *chocolate* digestives. Rolling out the red carpet for the weekend . . .

Ethan   Mum says, 'There's not nearly enough balloons in here. How about I open another huge packet?' but (*puffed out*) I can't – blow up – one – more – balloon –

Fiona   Seeya, Auntie Bev. Enjoy yourself! 'There's a party on this afternoon,' she says. 'Moira asked if you'd come down and help out. You remember Moira – big hair, bingo wings.' Course I remember Moira. She calls me Franny. (*Beat.*) My name's not Franny. 'They just need someone to hand out the fairy cakes and sausage rolls.' Sounds like the *worst use of a perfectly good Saturday ever.* 'She'll pay you five pounds.' I consider it before . . . 'No way.' But Auntie Bev says, 'I already said you'd do it.' I'm livid at that. 'I took you in when you were a teeny tiny baby,' she says, 'and this is the thanks I get? You're coming and that's the end of it.'

Fiona *sighs.*

Fiona   I bet Captain America never had to put up with this stuff. (*Beat.*) Community centre here I come.

Ethan   This place looks wicked!

Ethan *high-fives a long line of kids as they come through the door.*

Ethan   Hey – Yo – Nice – Cool – Hiya –

William   What am I doing here? We're supposed to be staying away from each other, not showing up at each other's parties . . .

Fiona   Sausage roll? Sausage roll?

Ethan   Thanks for coming – good to see you – drinks are on the counter, presents in the corner . . .

Fiona   Can I interest you in a chocolate krispy cake?

Ethan   William?!

William   My Dad made me come.

Ethan   And you couldn't say no?

William   I wanted to. Your Mum invited us.

Ethan   Right.

William   I guess he kept in touch with your Mum after . . .

Ethan   S'pose.

William   So we're here.

Ethan   Yup.

William   And it's my Dad so I can't just turn round and go home.

Ethan   Cos he'd say . . .

William   Ethan's Mum invited us and it'd be rude . . .

Ethan   I get it.

William   So we can stay?

Ethan *hesitates for a beat.*

Ethan   Drinks are on the counter, presents in the corner. And no freezing things, yeah, it's meant to be a party?

Fiona (*bright*)   Fairy cake?

Ethan   Don't tell me Mum invited you too?

Fiona   My Auntie Bev and Moira made me come.

Ethan *and* **William** *are drawing a blank.*

Ethan   I don't think I invited anyone called Auntie Bev or Moira . . .

Fiona   They work here. The ladies with the hairnets?

Ethan and **William** *immediately know who she's talking about.*

Ethan   Oh! So that's why you're . . .

Fiona   Hanging out with a tray full of sausages on sticks. Yeah, pretty much.

Ethan   So you're not going to go setting fires or anything then?

Fiona   Like I'd burn down the community centre. Auntie Bev would be hanging round the house every weekend if I did that. (*Beat.*) You stay out of my way and I'll stay out of yours.

Fiona *walks off.* **William** *hurries to catch her.*

William   My Mum used to make me read to old ladies at the care home.

Fiona *gives* **William** *a sideways look.*

William   So I know how you feel, is what I'm saying.

Fiona   No one knows how I feel.

William   She says it like she's the only one! Course no one knows how she feels! We're thirteen, we're not allowed to talk about real things, we don't I feel this, or I feel that. It's all football and pizza and have you seen this cat video? It's well funny! (*Beat.*) I used to be the same until Mum left. When she was around things were normal and I could just be a kid. Without her . . . It's hard to explain. Like, one minute there was carpet on the floor and the next it was gone. Not just the carpet, the whole floor. I could see this big black hole and there wasn't anything to stop me falling into it. And all I wanted to talk about was how I felt about things, but no one would listen. Not even Dad. And that was horrible.

Ethan   The party kicks off. Presents everywhere! Balloons everywhere!

Fiona   Half-trodden fairy cakes everywhere! Clean them up yourself, Auntie Bev!

William   I just hang out in the corner with Dad. They can keep their lame games of pass the parcel . . .

Ethan   I win pass the parcel! (*Beat.*) Mum wouldn't rig a game. Would she?

William   Musical statues. Keep well out the way.

Fiona   I'm almost glad I haven't been invited to this thing. Hasn't Ethan's Mum heard of bowling? Ice skating? DVDs even?

Ethan   I thought things had been going alright. Then Mum starts to get people up dancing . . .

Fiona   Ha! Cringe.

William   I'm not cool but even I know this party is *really* not cool.

Ethan   How did this happen?! Just when I think things can't get any worse, Mum goes over to William's Dad . . .

William   No. No, make it stop!

Ethan   'Would you care for this dance?' she says.

William   'Don't mind if I do.'

Fiona   This is like a hilarious car crash. They start swaying to the latest Justin Bieber. (*Beat.*) Then – out of nowhere –

William   There's a smash as something comes crashing through a window.

Ethan   Which is bad, but at least it makes them stop dancing.

Fiona   I've seen one of them before, of course.

Ethan   Everyone's seen a slug before, right?

Fiona   It's just that they're usually smaller.

William   Sticking to the side of a welly boot or something?

Ethan   And I don't think I've ever seen a slug with fangs before . . .

Fiona   It's flying through the air right towards us!!

Ethan   It can fly *and* it has fangs?!

William   This doesn't seem fair somehow . . . Quick, duck and cover!

William *does a forward roll just like when he's playing a video game.*

Fiona   It's still coming for us!

William   It isn't long before everyone else spots it too.

Fiona   Not a shocker really. We're talking a tonne of slug meat coming through the air like a dart.

William   Kids scream. Parents make the sort of faces people make when they really want to scream but feel they have to put a brave face on.

Fiona   Auntie Bev drops a whole tray full of sausage rolls and makes a 'baah!' sound.

Ethan   Everyone running with their hands in the air.

William   Diving under tables.

Fiona   Baah! Geroff! Eek!

Ethan   No one cares about the balloons anymore. Not even Mum.

William   Because stood right in front of everyone at the party is six foot of slug.

Fiona   'My name is Barbara,' says the slug. 'I am the most beautiful slug in the whole slug world.'

William   Are you sure, mate?

Ethan   Hang on. Are you a *girl*?

Fiona   'Human scum. Why do you always have to put us slug kind down, remove us from houses and kill us with horrid pellets the whole time?' Barbara continues. 'You lot are well nasty.'

William   We are not!

Fiona   'Are so!' Barbara says. There are great big strings of spit hanging from her slug mouth now and they go everywhere when she talks. 'The only things worse than humans are human children. I hate the lot of you! I'd happily see all the children in the whole wide world tied up in a big ball and bounced right off a cliff.'

Ethan   Well that's not very nice, is it?

Fiona   'Children are to slugs what dog poo is to pavements.'

William   Now you're just being mean!

Fiona   'Which is why when my mate The Darkness called me up . . .'

William   Hang on, Barbara . . .

Ethan   *Called* you? Called you on what?

William   Sure he didn't write you a letter? And send it via snail mail?

William *laughs at his own joke.*

Ethan   Dad jokes? Reckon now's a good time, do you?

William   You're right. Sorry.

Ethan   So this friend of yours, The Darkness, you say?

Fiona   'That's it,' Barbara says. 'And he did call me, actually. Us slugs are very technologically advanced. We've had mobile phones for almost six months and three days.'

William   What about e-mail?

Fiona   'Who's email?' says Barbara.

Ethan   So, anyway, this Darkness guy . . .

Fiona   'Big Evil critter. Big boss of all us evil underlings. Rang me up the other day and said, "I need a favour, Babs" and I said, "It'll cost you." So he paid me three and a half pence to kill the three special ones and here I am.'

William   Wow. So much wrong with that last sentence.

Ethan   No such thing as half a pence for a start.

Fiona   'Did I say half a pence? I meant a half eaten rolo. I love rolos, especially when they've been in someone else's gob for a few minutes.'

Ethan   Gross.

William   Plus – the special ones?

Fiona   'That would be you lot,' Barbara says. 'I hope so, anyway, or I'm in the wrong place and I can't give that rolo back.'

Ethan   Why is The Darkness after us?

William   What have we ever done to him?

Fiona   'I don't CARE!' Barbara roars. 'I came here to crunch you into teeny tiny pieces and that's what I'm going to do. I didn't have lunch because I was coming here – you people owe me a meal!'

Fiona   Party's over.

Ethan   People are shaking.

Fiona   All that stands between them and a big sluggy nightmare is –

William   Us.

Ethan   Three kids.

Fiona   Superpowers aren't all that when you've had them less than a week.

William   Goblins are one thing but she's –

Fiona   Massive!

William   A much bigger challenge.

Ethan   We could kill someone!

William   But if we do nothing, that giant slug will eat every child in the room.

Fiona   She's *drooling* at the thought of it.

William   She'll munch through them like chicken wings.

Ethan   Bones thrown in the corner piling up and up and up.

Fiona   It's down to us.

Ethan   We're all there is.

William   Could go wrong.

Fiona   Has to go right.

William   Where are we going to find the world's biggest slug pellet?

Ethan   Maybe if I shake the ground really hard she'll fall down and we can tie her up?

William   Her body's got to be at least part water. I can freeze her from the inside out.

Fiona   Cook her. Make her eyes pop like corn.

Ethan   All three of us try.

Fiona   Focused and determined.

William   Summoning our superpowers from the depths of our souls. And –

Ethan/Fiona/William   Ahh!

Fiona   'Incoming!' yells Babs.

Ethan   Incoming what?

Fiona   Barbara shoots slime out her nostril and it lands in big blobs everywhere.

Ethan   Right, now I get it.

William   That is seriously gross!

Ethan   Everything's covered! Make it stop!

Fiona   So much for superpowers!

William   Then I get an idea . . . I fix my mind on the sea. The idea of it. The smell of it. The vast bodies of water and the salt that lies within it.

Ethan   Wait a minute. Salt. Doesn't that . . .?

William   That's the plan.

Fiona   So get on with it then!

William   I concentrate. I summon the sea to bend to my will!

Ethan   Salt water starts shooting through the windows!

William   It's working!

Fiona   Keep going!

Ethan   The whole community centre fills with the smell of sea air.

William   And Babs goes . . .

Fiona   'Salt is to slugs what broccoli is to children! We mustn't be exposed to it! We can't stand it! We – Ahhh!'

Ethan   Her eyes start bulging out of her head!

William   Her body starts going fizzzzz . . .

Fiona   'I'm melting!' says Barbara, melting. 'You'll regret this you little munchkins! You might get the best of Babs but you'll never beat The Darkness!'

Ethan   Big words from a slug who's about to become a puddle.

Fiona   'When you see The Darkness, and you will . . .' says Barbara, 'tell him Babs said to . . .'

William   Barbara melts into a big gooey, stinky puddle before she can even finish her sentence.

Ethan   We won!

Fiona   I'm about to do a victory dance when –

William   We turn around and everyone's looking at us.

Ethan   Mum's got this terrified look on her face. She's also got quite a lot of Barbara in her hair.

Fiona   Auntie Bev's staring at me like she doesn't know who I am anymore. She's looking at the massive puddle of slug goo. 'Who's going to clean this up then?' she says.

William   I can tell exactly what Dad's thinking. 'That gargoyle wasn't a dream, was it?' he says.

Ethan   All the kids I've invited to my party, that were playing pass the parcel and musical statues a few minutes ago are just standing there with their mouths open. 'Was that real?' they say.

Fiona   'All those things you did,' Moira says. 'How did you do it, Fanny?'

William   So many questions.

Ethan   Like we have any more answers than they do . . .

Fiona   There's no point denying it anymore, is there? So I say, it happened on my birthday.

William   Superpowers.

Ethan   Don't know how.

Fiona   Or why.

William   Or how long it'll last.

Ethan   But yeah.

Beat.

Fiona   Surprise!

William   We don't give people much time to get their head round things.

Ethan   Cos it's pretty clear to everyone that we've got bigger things to worry about.

Fiona   Cos this stuff keeps happening to us.

William   There's been three gargoyles and a goblin, a giant slug with massive fangs –

Ethan   All out to get us.

Fiona   Pretty unlucky.

William   Not luck. A plan.

Ethan   But why?

Fiona   'Cos you're superheroes, duh?' says Connor Pike, who's on the football team.

Ethan   'And they all know that,' my Mum pipes up.

William   'It's like the slug said,' Dad goes. 'They work for the same guy.'

Fiona   'The Darkness, that's what he said, isn't it?' says Auntie Bev.

William   Doesn't sound like a human name.

Fiona   'The Darkness.' Sounds creepy.

Ethan   Probably not a person.

William   Could be anything.

Fiona   Emphasis on the *thing* part.

Ethan   Cos what sort of critter is the leader of a gang that includes gargoyles –

William   Goblins.

Fiona   And ugly bugly slugs?

Ethan   Whoever The Darkness is, they've got to be bad –

William   Mad.

Fiona   Dangerous.

Ethan   And he's after us.

William   The question is – why?

Fiona   Maybe it's all about sizzle, freeze, shake?

Ethan   'You're targets because you're strong,' Mum suggests.

William   'Because something's happening to you that you don't understand,' Dad says.

Fiona   'You're being attacked now while you're still weak. While you're still learning how to use your powers,' says Auntie Bev.

Ethan   Just throwing this out there, but any chance we could chat about this while we eat cake? Sort of missing my own birthday party here . . .

William   But there's no time to even think about cake, because the next second –

Fiona   BOOM BOOM BOOM.

Ethan   Footsteps. And –

William   SWISH SWISH SWISH.

Ethan   Sounds like a . . . tail?

Fiona   A dragon smashes through one wall of the community centre.

William   More screaming.

Fiona   Auntie Bev dives behind some pick and mix.

Ethan   The dragon lurches through what used to be a wall and is now a massive hole.

William   I can't imagine there's such a thing as a small dragon, but this is a –

Fiona   Very. Big. Dragon.

Ethan   It snatches up my Mum in one of its clawed hands. Mum!

William   Dad! It's got him too!

Fiona   Auntie Bev's hiding. (*Hissing.*) Keep. Down!

Ethan   He's getting away! Stop him!

William   Dad's kicking out but he can't get free.

Fiona   The dragon grabs Auntie Bev. All I can think about is how many times I've wished she wasn't my Auntie and now . . .

Ethan   Don't worry, Mum! I'll think of something!

William   I'm coming for you, Dad!

Fiona (*to* **Auntie Bev**)   I'm sorry. Don't hate me. I love you.

Ethan   Stomp stomp as the dragon crushes the broken glass under his feet as he goes and then – silence.

Ethan   What are we going to do now?!

William   Easy. Find them and stop the dragon.

Fiona   You did notice the word dragon in that sentence?

William   They have our families. What choice do we have?

Fiona   None.

William   We need a plan.

Ethan   Give me one minute. I'll think of something.

Fiona   I think you mean 'we'?

Ethan   Err, nope. Think I was right the first time.

Fiona   What, because you're automatically the leader?

William   Unbelievable!

Ethan   Come on. I've got experience. Social skills. I've been captain of the football team three years running!

Fiona   Remind me to fashion you a medal when we get out of here.

Ethan   I know how to lead. Whereas you two . . .

William   It was me that got rid of Barbara the giant slug lady.

Fiona   And if it wasn't for my fire power we'd never have got that goblin out of detention.

William   All you've done so far is make people fall down a lot.

Ethan   Well someone has to be in charge. Do you want to find your Dad and Auntie Bev or not?

William   If this wasn't a life or death situation I would so have given him a piece of my mind . . .

Fiona   Cos could he be more annoying?

William   Still. No time to argue when there's a terrifying dragon on the loose.

Fiona   Plus Ethan's the only one who thinks he knows where the dragon might have taken everyone.

Ethan   Hand to the ground. I can feel the dragon's footsteps through the soil. Something I can track.

William   So we follow him. Still not agreeing he's the leader, though . . .

Ethan   We follow the dragon all the way through town –
over the shaky bridge and down an alleyway I've never been
down before. At the end, there's a disused warehouse.

William   I get to the door. Ear to the wood. Inside –
muffled sounds. People crying. Wimpering. And in the
middle of it all – heavy breathing.

Fiona   I peer through a crack in the door. The warehouse is
big and damp, like a cave. Old boxes everywhere, rubbish
lying on the floor.

Ethan   I can see Mum, William's Dad, and Fiona's Auntie
Bev cowering against a far wall, and there, in the middle of it
all, right in front of me is a huge, scaly, living, breathing
dragon.

William   The dragon must be The Darkness! Has to be.
He's sat there picking something out his teeth with a twisty
claw. And his *breath*. It smells like rotting fish and cheesy feet
all rolled into one gross bundle.

Ethan   All the gargoyles and goblins and giant slugs in the
world are nothing compared to this! I look down at my
knees. They're shaking. I'm scared. Terrified.

Fiona   There's a dragon on the other side of this door and I
don't think we can handle it.

William   The dragon speaks. 'Little children. Little
children out there?'

Ethan   Can he smell us?

William   'Do you know who I am, little children? What my
name is? Why I'm here? Why *you* are here?'

Ethan   I close my eyes. Squeeze them shut.

William   'Have you ever seen a dragon before, little
children?'

Ethan   He *definitely* has to be The Darkness. I can feel his
hot breath through the door.

William   'I bet you have lots of questions, little children. Like, why did this happen to me? Why has he come after me? *How am I going to die?*'

Fiona   Oh this is so bad . . .

William   'Which one of you is the leader?' says the dragon.

Fiona   He is!

Ethan   Shhh!

Fiona   Let me guess. Not so keen on the whole leader thing now?

Ethan   Look, I'm sorry, alright. I shouldn't have tried to take over, but please don't make me go in there and face that dragon on my own!

William   Course not.

Fiona   That would be well harsh if we made you do that.

William   What we waiting for then?

Fiona   We rush the door. I shoot fire from my fingers as I run inside.

William   Freeze ray from my eyes –

Ethan   I hit the dirt. Trying to disrupt the earth the dragon's standing on.

Fiona   The fire bounces right off his big scaly bonce!

William   A sheet of ice hits him. Smashes. It's not working!

Ethan   He's standing firm. There's nothing I can do!

Fiona   The dragon rears up, leans over us –

William   Teeth glistening –

Ethan   Venom dribbling –

Fiona   Hot breath.

William   Evil little smile.

Ethan   The dragon laughs at us. His cackle echoing round the room.

William (*cackle*)   'Don't you know who I am?' he asks. 'My name is Fergus, born of fire. I have been loyal to The Darkness for thousands of years and I will be loyal to The Darkness for thousands more. You, little children, are insignificant to me.'

Fiona   Superhero huddle?

Fiona, **William** *and* **Ethan** *huddle up.*

William   So he's not The Darkness then?

Ethan   Fergus. Weird name for a dragon.

Fiona   Not to mention, if we're so insignificant, then why is he here?

William   Why did he kidnap our families?

Fiona   He must know who we are. How we got these powers. And why.

Ethan   Plus, he knows that we can stop him.

Fiona   Right, except we couldn't. Our powers bounced right off him.

William   He laughed in our superhero faces.

Ethan   Yeah but that was before.

William   Before what?

Ethan   Before we worked together. (*To* **Fiona**.) You were right. I've been horrible.

Fiona   Well, lucky for you we're better people.

William   Plus we all make mistakes, right?

Fiona   I don't. I'm always right. It's a gift. (*Beat.*) Maybe that's one of my superpowers?

Ethan   I cared more about being captain of the team than being myself. (*To* **William**.) We've known each other since we were small. *Course* we're mates. (*To* **Fiona**.) And I've always known who you are.

Fiona   Really?

Ethan   I don't know why I pretended. Except that . . .

William   It's not easy being thirteen.

Ethan *nods*.

Fiona   Not to interrupt this really touching moment or anything but . . . I spy with my little eye something beginning with big hairy dragon?

Ethan   Right.

William   Knew there was something we had to do . . .

Ethan   So we work together then.

Fiona   Join forces.

William   Like we're linked.

Fiona   Fire.

William   Ice.

Ethan   *And* tremor. All together.

Fiona   All at once.

William   All focused on *him*.

Fiona   That way he won't have time to stop each power. When he tries to fight fire –

William   He'll be hit with ice. And when he tries to lash out at the ice –

Ethan   The earth beneath his feet will give way.

Fiona   He might be able to take us on one at a time. But he can't fight us all at once.

William   We strike a superhero stance –

Fiona   I prep my fire balls –

William   Freeze ray on!

Ethan   Contact made with the earth and –

Fiona   Fire!

Ethan   Tremors!

William   Ice!

Ethan   He rears up and screams.

William   'You've never gone up against a dragon before have you, little children? But of course. You've never really gone up against anyone before.'

Fiona   You're not a one, mate, you're a thing.

Ethan   And we've been up against plenty.

Fiona   You keep forgetting. *We're thirteen.*

Ethan/Fiona/William   Tremor! Ice! Fire!

Ethan   The dragon shakes his head from side to side.

William   'No!' he says. 'Stop. What are you doing?!'

Ethan   And I say back to his ugly mug, 'What we should have done ages ago!'

Ethan/Fiona/William   Sizzle! Freeze! Shake!

William   What we're going to do all the time from now on.

Ethan/Fiona/William   Roast! Shiver! Tremble!

William   'You're hurting me!' he cries.

Fiona   Get out of our town, dragon features!

Ethan   You're not the law around here.

Ethan/Fiona/William   Scorch! Cool! Quake!

William   He screeches. He flails.

Fiona   Dragon in a tailspin.

Ethan   Dragon in a daze.

Fiona   He's covered in hot boils from my fire.

William   Icicles hanging from his feet.

Ethan   And I shake shake shake him until he doesn't know which way is up.

Fiona   He's spinning round and round and round.

William   His wings stretch out from the side of his body. They're huge!

Fiona   He flaps his wings . . .

Ethan   And SMASH! He punches his way through the roof.

William   'The Darkness will hear about this,' he says. 'You'll regret the very day you were born!' and he flies off.

Ethan   We've done it!

William   Whoop for joy!

Fiona   An extra-special, all-caution-to-the-wind victory dance!

Fiona *does a pimped-up victory dance.*

Fiona   Everyone seems pretty grateful when we rescue them.

Ethan   Mum says I'm the best superhero out the three of us. (*Beat.*) I tell her it was a team effort.

William   Dad hugs me tighter than he has in a long time. He even tells me he loves me.

Fiona   Auntie Bev gets well mushy.

Ethan   'Congratulations, children.' A voice says out of nowhere. 'You have done even better than I thought you might.'

William   Who is *that?*

Fiona   Has to be The Darkness . . .

Ethan   'Well done,' says the voice. 'Now follow me. What I have to say is not for the ears of mere mortals.'

Fiona   We can't see you, how are we supposed to follow you?!

Ethan   'Do you feel that chill in the air?' says the voice.

William   I thought that was just me.

Ethan   'And that foul smell on the breeze?'

Fiona   I thought that was just him.

Ethan   'Now follow it. And do not stop until I tell you or you'll never see these people you call family again.'

William   So what are we supposed to do?

Fiona   Only one thing we can do.

Ethan   We follow.

William   Don't worry, Dad.

Ethan   We'll be back, Mum.

Fiona   Just hang tight, Auntie Bev.

William   We go out of the warehouse.

Fiona   Across the road with the traffic lights that take ages.

Ethan   Past our school.

William   Near the bus stop where I last saw Mum.

Fiona   Finally we get to the town square.

Ethan   The green where kids play games and grown-ups sit on benches to chat or read the paper.

William   Where the big sycamore tree stands in the middle.

Fiona   So, Mr The Darkness, if that is in fact your real name –

William   'It is, in fact, my real name,' says the voice.

Fiona   Where are you and what are you and why have you dragged us out here to the middle of the green?

William   'I brought you here to give you a choice,' it says.

Fiona   A choice about which way we're going to die, by any chance?

Ethan   'On the contrary,' he says. 'A choice about how you're going to live. Since you turned thirteen, a lot has changed, has it not?'

William   He knows about our powers!

Fiona   'I gave you your powers,' the voice says. 'Or at least, you have them because of me. What I didn't know was whether you were worthy of them. Which is why I sent some of my more colourful friends to test you.'

William   But why? What have we ever done to you?

Fiona   Show yourself, coward!

Ethan   We're not as defenceless as we look!

William   Just ask those creatures you sent if you don't believe us.

Fiona   'Oh I believe you,' says the voice, a little sadly. 'No children of mine would ever be defenceless.'

Ethan   Well.

Fiona   I mean, what were we supposed to say to *that*?

William   You're a liar.

Ethan   Total liar.

Fiona   The three of us aren't even related.

Ethan   'But you are,' the voice says. 'You are all my children – triplets – each adopted by a separate family. That's why you feel such a powerful link to one another. I know you've felt it.'

Fiona   So what if we have? It doesn't mean we feel anything for you.

Ethan   'I am all the things that keep you up at night. Everything that is difficult or unfair in the world is me. I was made to destroy – to be the mould on the bread and the rust on the bicycle wheel.'

Beat.

Fiona   Don't you sound charming.

William   So you can't be our Dad. We've all made mistakes but we're nothing like you.

Ethan   We're good people.

William   Kind.

Fiona   At least one of us is funny.

William   We couldn't be less like you if we tried.

Ethan   'That is what I feared,' The Darkness mutters. 'I worried that you would inherit my powers but not my spirit. But when you killed my gargoyles and tortured the goblin, salted the slug and attacked the dragon, I knew I had my answer. You are just like I am.'

Fiona   But we only did those things out of self defence!

Ethan   'The incidents at school weren't self-defence,' he says. 'You did those things for fun. Someone could easily have gotten burned on hot pizza, broke a leg on a football pitch of ice or hurt themselves when the earth shook them to the ground.'

Fiona   Yeah but we didn't *mean* to hurt anyone.

William   'Together, we will have a dark future. Just like the rest of the planet,' The Darkness tells us.

Ethan   I don't understand.

Fiona   'Humans are worthless,' The Darkness groans. 'They are selfish and pointless and weak. When there are no more people, we will have the run of the place, just like it was before. Ethan, you can create earthquakes to level cities and bury civilizations. Fiona, your fire can lay waste to entire continents with a click of your fingers. William can make the sea rise and the ice caps melt. Together, you have the power to destroy every living creature on the planet. (*Beat.*) I am so proud of you all.'

William   We're superheroes, mate, not super-idiots!

Ethan   What about our Mums and Dads and Aunties?

Fiona   'They will be erased like pencil from the pages of history,' The Darkness says.

Ethan   We'd never do any of the stuff you just talked about.

Fiona   You've got the wrong triplets.

William   'Oh dear,' The Darkness says. 'In that case, this is where you say goodbye.'

Ethan   There's a rumbling under our feet.

William   Dark clouds gather above our heads.

Fiona   And lightning starts crackling all around.

Ethan   Until all that electricity gathers into three giant forks.

William   One for each of us. And we realize –

Fiona   The Darkness has powers of his own! If we won't join him he's going to kill us where we stand!

Ethan   Not if I have anything to do with it. (*Shouting.*) The Darkness! Listen to me!

Fiona   Nothing.

Ethan   I don't give up. (*Shouting.*) I know you think we're a threat to you but that only works if we're all together. That's the only way we could defeat the dragon. Which means, you only have to kill one of us. And I think that one should be me.

William   What are you doing?!

Ethan (*shouting*)   I'm the selfish one! I'm the one who thinks he's better than other people! I should be the one to die, just don't hurt William and Fiona!

Fiona   Hang on, don't we get a say in this?

William   I'm not going to let my brother get hurt, not for anything. (*Shouting.*) Take me! I'm the one you should kill!

Fiona   Do you mind? (*Shouting.*) I've only just found my brothers! It's the first club I've ever belonged to and the only one I want to be in. Kill me! Just let them live!

Ethan   The earth shakes and the trees sway.

Fiona   The temperature drops like a stone.

William   You can taste the rot in the air.

Ethan   The lightning shoots down at us from above. We try and prepare for the worst.

Fiona   I close my eyes.

William   Think about Mum and Dad.

Ethan   I wish I could think of something special to say in the last few seconds of our lives!

Fiona   We brace ourselves and then –

William   Nothing.

Ethan   I open one eye . . .

Fiona   We're still alive!

William   Err, so what just happened?

Ethan   Suddenly, The Darkness appears right in front of us.

William   So not what I expected.

Fiona   He's not a creature at all.

William   He looks just like a normal bloke.

Ethan   Pretty tall –

Fiona   Good hair.

William   And the weirdest bit is he looks a bit like *us*.

Ethan   My eyes.

Fiona   My nose.

William   And those ears are a dead ringer for mine.

Ethan   He speaks to us.

William   'When you were born, I could see the good in you,' he says. 'I knew there was nothing but evil in me. That's why I gave you up – so you could find your own way in the world. But as the years went on, I missed you and hoped we could be together again. Hoped you would turn out evil like me. I see now that isn't the case.'

Ethan   Cos we've been brought up better than that.

Fiona   Auntie Bev's not perfect but she doesn't stand for evil in her house.

William   'I was right to leave you,' The Darkness says. 'There is nothing but darkness in my heart. Darkness – and the three of you.'

Ethan   And with that –

Fiona   He was gone as quickly as he'd appeared.

Ethan   So why aren't we dead?

William   The next minute Dad and Ethan's Dad and Fiona's Auntie Bev came running across the green towards us.

Ethan   'We thought we'd find you here,' says Mum. 'It's where we found you the first time.'

Fiona   Obviously we have some questions for them.

William   Like what happened to us?

Fiona   Where did you find us?

Ethan   Mum sat me down.

Fiona   Auntie Bev explains.

William   Dad says he wants to be honest for once.

Ethan   I wasn't adopted in the usual way like she'd always told me.

Fiona   There was a big storm. The sycamore tree in the middle of the green got struck by lightning.

William   For hours the wind howled.

Ethan   So bad that no one could leave their homes or even put their wheelie bins out.

Fiona   And when it died down –

William   While most people were counting their chimney pots and making sure no garden furniture had gotten blown over –

Ethan   In the middle of the green, next to what was left of the tree . . . was the three of us.

Fiona   Babies.

William   Defenceless.

Ethan   And all alone.

Fiona   So they took us in.

William   Cared for us.

Ethan   Loved and nurtured us.

Fiona   Treated us like their own.

William   Because we *were* their own.

Ethan   Some families don't start in the usual way, that's all.

Fiona   Like the three of us.

William   Who seemed to come from the centre of the earth.

Fiona   Like we were forged from fire.

William   Sprung from water.

Ethan   Grown in the earth.

Fiona   Gifts to three families who needed us and didn't even realize it.

William   Because sometimes you don't know what you need until it's right in front of you.

Ethan   And sometimes not even then.

Fiona   Like brothers.

William   Sisters.

Ethan   And friends.

Fiona   They have a theory about why we survived The Darkness's attack.

William   It's our love for each other.

Ethan   By trying to sacrifice ourselves for each other, we've all been saved.

Fiona   So from now on, if anything bad ever comes to kill us –

William   Or we come across something we're afraid we can't defeat.

Ethan   We know we can get through it. That working together is better than working alone.

William   No matter how small we seem.

Ethan   Or weak.

Fiona   Or young.

William   We care about each other now, which means that nothing bad can hurt us.

Ethan   We just have to remember that we're on the same side, that's all.

Fiona   No matter how different we might think we are.

Auntie Bev takes a cake out of her bag.

Ethan   Mum is singing. (*Singing.*) 'Happy Birthday to you . . .'

William   Dad, what are you doing?!

Fiona   Err, he's singing too?

William (*singing*)   'Happy Birthday to you . . .'

Ethan   Your Auntie Bev's joining in too!

Fiona (*singing*)   'Happy Birthday to William, Fiona and Ethan . . .' (*Beat.*) This is well embarrassing . . .

All (*singing*)   'Happy Birthday to you!'

Ethan, **Fiona** and **William** *look at each other for a beat.*

Ethan   Weirdest birthday ever, yeah?

William   Pretty much.

Fiona   It's been right up there with the time Auntie Bev promised to take me to Disneyland and we ended up in Weston-super-Mare.

Ethan   Still, it's been a lot of fun, though.

Fiona   That woman really needs to learn to read a bus timetable . . .

William   So listen. When we go back to school tomorrow –

Ethan   And everyone's talking about the party of the century.

Fiona   With its big ugly gatecrasher that tried to eat everyone right up.

William   Are we going to go back to pretending we're just normal thirteen year olds?

Beat.

Fiona   Why bother with all that?

Ethan   Seems a bit daft really.

Fiona   Honesty is the best policy, isn't it? Fire!

Ethan   Earth!

William   Water!

Party music kicks in. **Ethan**, **William** *and* **Fiona** *dance together, enjoying their weirdest birthday and getting to know each other properly at last.*

The End.

Printed in the USA
CPSIA information can be obtained
at www.ICGtesting.com
LVHW020938171024
794056LV00003B/836